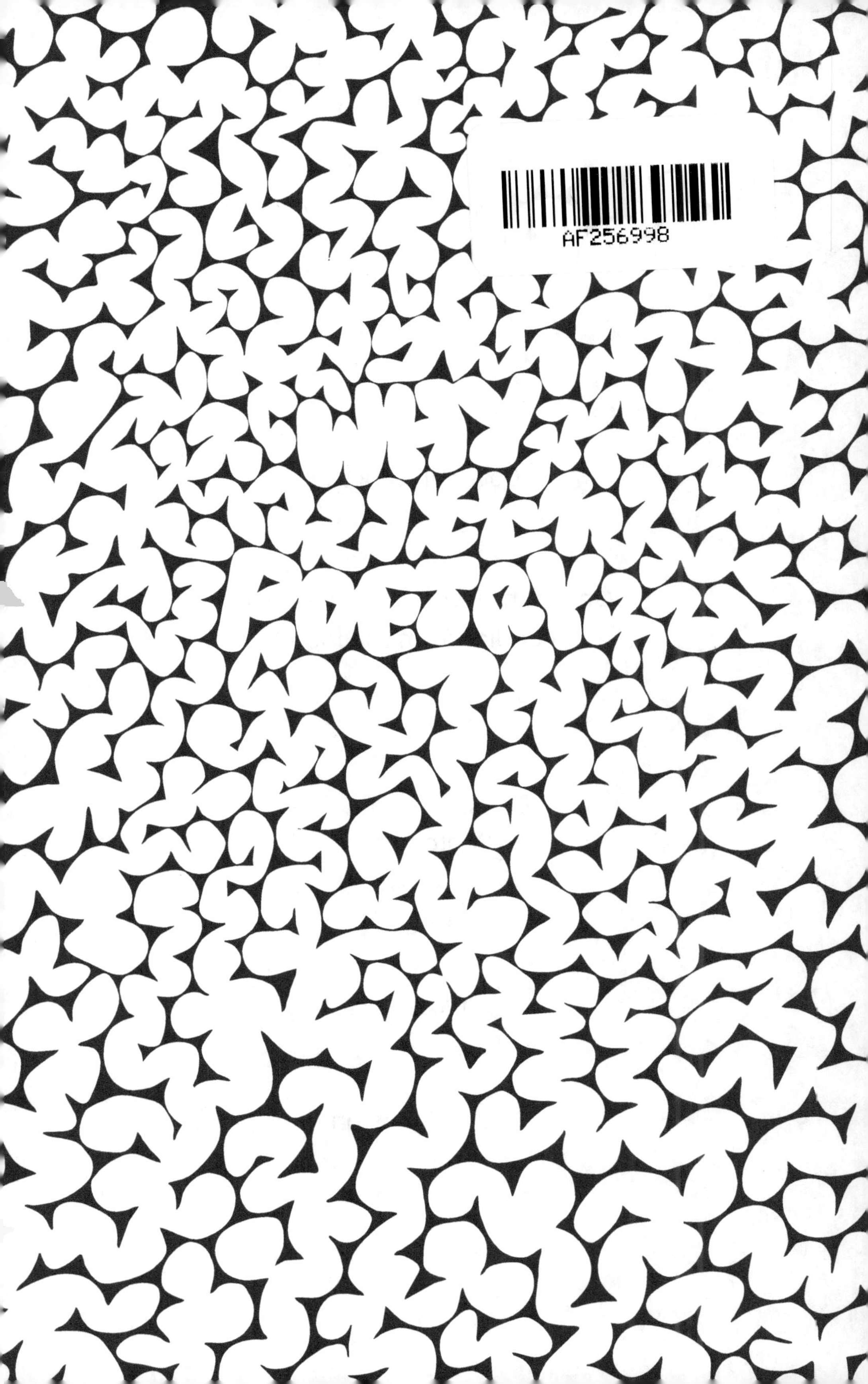

AF256998
WHY
POETRY?

Cover drawings by
Nigel Johnston

One of my favourite 'time-wasting'
doodles from childhood.

"Brains"


Photographs:
'Robin'
'Bridge'
'Lion'
'Waterfall'


by
Nigel Johnston

# Why Poetry?

Tales of autism
from behind the mask.

The poems of
**Nigel Johnston**

**Liane Matthews**
Drew the pictures

# Why Poetry?
## Tales of autism from behind the mask

Copyright © 2022 Nigel Johnston



*Published 25 May 2022 by Nigel Johnston*

ISBN: 978-1-7396772-0-6

Visit the author's website at

www.nigeljohnston.com

For Iona

When I had no words
You sat with me and listened

# Foreword

Iona, my occupational therapist at the time, suggested that if I ever published these poems, I should foreword them with some cautionary advice.

Poetry became a therapeutic tool for me; a way to express thoughts and experiences which, until then, had been buried by history and silence.

Whilst I have refrained from using profanity * the subject material does include themes of mental health issues, such as depression, homelessness, suicide, and other fun stuff.

These are tales of autism from behind the mask. I have tried to cover each topic as I view it, in a matter-of-fact manner and as concisely as possible. This may come across as 'blunt' on occasions.

I think that's what she meant.

Either that or it's just bad poetry.

** Apart from the word 'shit' in "Why Poetry?"*
*But it was unavoidable.*

# Contents

# Contents Continued

# Introduction

## "Oh..! Am I a poet..?"

...Was the question that struck me one day, after I'd returned to Lake House to begin another round of therapy sessions.

Faced with the prospect of having to remember and repeat the same stories, and open up all of the old wounds to another round of strangers, I figured it would save time and misunderstanding if I were to write everything down as a sort of 'story of me'.

I couldn't do it.

Memories of past events and experiences flooded my thoughts, there was no way I could write any of it down in a coherent sentence, let alone a story.

I was in a downward spiral, and a torrent of such recollections tainted anything from being good. I wasn't sleeping or eating. I had to get this information to the doctors, and quickly.

From the words I'd already scribbled down, I managed to rearrange them into what would become 'Train Wreck'. It sort of told a story, but had a broken rhythm to it.

From the original garbled attempt at writing an essay, I found that if I concentrated on each 'topic' individually and separately, ignoring the cries of the others, I could focus on the feelings they aroused and, for the first time, really explore them. Then all I had to do was find the words and form each one into a short, self-contained poem. In many cases, this took months.

The effect was cathartic. I'd found a voice.

By the time I was referred to Lake House my world had imploded and my body was tearing itself apart. Anything and anybody beyond the single room of my small flat was too much for me to cope with. A lifetime of masking and faulty coping mechanisms had finally caught up with me.

I got lucky.

When I broke down in her office, Amanda, my GP, handled it perfectly. I will forever be in awe and moved by the power of her concern, compassion, and professionalism.

At Lake House, I was assigned an occupational therapist. One of the first things Iona said to me was "You're not broken". All I could do was smile at her because I knew I was, but I admired her optimism. And so it began. She talked, I listened. I broke my silence with fumbled words, she listened. The poems in this book were written during, and are a direct result of, the therapy sessions with Iona.

When I half-jokingly brought up the possibility of publishing this poetry in a book (and if you're reading this, it has become reality) she was initially concerned. I would be 'opening up' for the world to see.

However, none of these situations, thoughts, emotions, are unique to me. Writing them as poetry made me slow down and re-examine, with a deliberate focus on, life's hardships and also life's achievements. It is a worthy therapeutic tool that I can wholeheartedly recommend.

If a poem can say what you cannot, that is progress.

So..! Am I a poet?

Well, no. That wasn't it.

All of this had me thinking back to the poets I'd learned about in school (and the ones I hadn't) and the abundance of mental health and other difficulties they'd each suffered and endured, including many suicides.

"Oh...!"

Along with that, it was the way they looked at the world and were able to articulate their thoughts, emotions, and experiences. There is a unique, expressive power in poetry. In the midst of tragedy and despair, they found beauty.

What follows are just some of my experiences, thoughts, and observations, from a time before the issues of autism were really an issue.

Some of it rhymes.

Nigel

Why Poetry?

# Why Poetry?

"Why poetry?"
And then, 'the look'.
The one that's guaranteed.
"I've got to read those poncey lines?"
"It don't mean shit to me!"

Yet, in amongst that poncey shit,
And all those fiddly, rhyming bits,
You'll find a map, to an address,
In metaphor to help express,
A deeper context to the words,
That never had the chance of birth.

The intricacies of the mind,
The layers laying intertwined,
Exposed in prose for all to find.
But mainly,
It's for me.

# Growing Up

As a child, they'd always ask,
"What do you want to be?"
I found this odd, you see, because,
I was already,
Me.

And as an adolescent,
I missed a year of school.
Though I taught myself,
The things I thought,
Revealed revealing clues,
To what this world was all about,
And where I fitted in.
I learnt to learn those lessons absent,
From that Looney bin.

But older is as older gets,
And time sometimes contains regrets,
As Life is lost to loneliness,
Because of being me.

# Parties

*A party invitation,*
*Répondez S'il Vous Plaît,*
*We'd love for you to join us,*
*& celebrate this day.*


Such an innocent request,
Belies within, a hidden test.
A trial which I must endure,
Because I'm rude if I ignore.

It means a lot, you thought of me,
I know I'm not great company,
So please don't think that I don't care,
Just in case I can't be there.
I love you deeply; everyone,
But overwhelming numbers numb,
And all the masks in which I hide,
In close proximity, collide.

It's not the same as being shy,
Or bothersome belly butterflies.
It isn't fear of anything,
It's just my dodgy wiring.
It causes me to overload,
I have to ground to gain control.

I'll be the guest in need of rest,
If I accept, this hidden test.

# Train Wreck

A Train of thought,
A fast moving, fully laden, diesel powered freight train.
No-one cares to ride this train,
Yet it contains equipment; machinery; interesting stuff.
Lots of inertia; Loads of momentum.
It's Marvellous; Unstoppable!
Everyone is happy!

I never see what derails it.

I'm at the scene of this enormous mess.

Carriages, engines, tracks, cargo; listing, scattered and twisted.
Wreckage amid desolation.
Everyone is looking.

I try to pick a few bits up.

Everyone is waiting.

# Occupational Therapy

At thirteen I was sent to see,
A doctor of psychology.
Not for breaking any rules,
Just choosing freedom, over school.

But déjà vu, it seems I'm back,
The same, familiar attacks,
The fall and subsequent collapse,
With such a heavy toll.

For everything before has failed,
(From medicines to booze)
And doctors lose their patience,
When their questions just confuse.

Yet this time, with a friendly voice,
And friendly ear to match,
I think we're getting nearer,
To the itch behind the scratch.

For many folk have felt this way,
For many years before.
They'd lose their minds or lose themselves,
In art and literature.

Expression comes in many forms,
So find your form and show it,
With paint or clay, or maybe you'll say,
"Oh..! Am I a poet?"

# Avoidance

Avoidance!
When you said that word,
Those little sparks of thoughts occurred.
They formed a shape, it span around,
And action transformed, into noun.
So off I went on some absurd,
Journey into self.

Do you avoid these?
Tick the box:

The Park          ☑
The Bank          ☑
The Pub           ☑
The Shops         ☑

Always looking for the clocks,
To make a quick escape?

As action transformed, into noun,
I caught myself, looking down.
And there I was with no disguise,
No alcohol, no alibis.
The awkwardness exposed to see.
I've only been, avoiding me.

# Just Call

"Just call me if you need me."
A lovely phrase to hear,
"If you're having troubles,
The phone is always near."

But that's a thing I cannot do,
I don't have any words for you,
And while my mind is primed to burst,
My silence only makes it worse.

This mutism is quite unique,
On other subjects I can speak,
Freely and with competence,
(Occasionally with confidence)
But if the topic takes a turn,
I can't describe my own concerns.

And that just helps to make belief,
That everything's alright with me,
But veiled by this secrecy,
My world's falling apart.

*Only very recently,*
*I've found a voice, in poetry.*

# Depression

Get up! Get dressed!
Stop saying that. I really wish you would.
Get up! Get dressed!
I'm telling you, I'm just not in the mood.

Get up, get dressed, and go outside.
It's beautiful today.
Just think of all the things you'll miss.
It's such a crying shame.

I can't do that. I know I can.
I argue with myself.
And while this battle wages on,
It's costing me my health.

Get up! Get dressed!
For pity's sake, I wish I'd shut my face!
This mission of attrition greets,
The dawn of every day.

# Withdraw

Every day, I'm finding more
And more I've closed another door.
Find a place to hide,
Withdraw,
As cries and even pleas remain,
Ignored.

# Lethargic

This lethargy is

Photograph - 'Robin'


A quiet walk in nature brings a sense of calmness and belonging.

I watched a little robin hopping,
Back and forth from bush to tree.
I watched him 'til I realised,
That really, he was watching me.

# Insomniac Dreams

As King Kong grabbed me in his paw,
Dripping fangs to frame his fearsome roar,
It caused my sleeping, childhood eyes,
To snap to life,
To realise,
Such nightmares meant,
I'd been asleep,
The first time for,
So many weeks.

*As often,*
*Long throughout the night,*
*I'd lay awake,*
*Aware of that,*
*Nocturnal state,*
*As limbs and lungs and stomach too,*
*Would shake and dance to some,*
*Disjointed tune.*

In due course,

Darkness turned to dawn,

To thoughts of school,

And uniforms.

A day of battles lay ahead,

Without the benefit of bed,

Without recourse,

Without respite,

With just the fear to face at night,

Where troubled thinking congregates,

And turns to dreams of,

Giant,

Terrifying Apes.

# Nice Dreams

A sunny summer's day, grass vivid green,
Amid the rolling hills arranged to set the scene,
When to the left, it caught my eye,
A placid lake reflecting hues to match the sky.
The air was warm, and so I strolled,
Towards the water which I sensed would quench my soul.

But then I stopped.
With a start.
With a rapid, elevating rate of heart.
Around the distant water's edge,
Appeared a trail of dots, defying any sense,
For they just bobbed above the ground,
With gentle undulations.
Then the Sound!

*Triumphal music from above.*
*Swept away on waves of post-euphoric love.*

And so I knew,
These distant points contained a clue,
A hidden message for some mission yet to do?
And as the first came into view,
I saw such carvings cutting, intricately through.

Beside this lake, in a field of dreams,

Before my eyes, this orb transformed into a 'T'.

The next an 'H',

And then an 'E',

A sudden surge of subdued, timeless memories.


So there I stood,

A growing smile,

A row of letters, floating, echoing for miles.


The message here and clearly shown;


T H E Y ' R E   C O M I N G


We are not alone.

COMING THE
ERYEHT GN I
THE

# Social Bluff

"Hello you, how've you been?"
"Had a busy week?"
I'm quite the social creature,
(He says, with tongue-in-cheek)

It's no surprise, these lines I've learned,
Delivered with aplomb,
Would ever lead you to believe,
That anything is wrong.

But everything's on high alert,
Adrenalin on tap.
These signals I must override,
This isn't an attack.

And while I force this fear to fade,
And keep a grip on this cascade,
Of information flooding in,
I still maintain a stupid grin,
And hope that I have done enough,
To navigate this social bluff.

Although I know it doesn't show,
These shallow words hide depths below.
Emotions few will ever feel,
Forged from nerves of shattered steel.
The bonds that link me to the past,
Are transient, they never last.

Like flotsam on an empty beach,
Cast away,
Out of reach.

# The Spian

Want to watch a movie?
Sit back, relax, enjoy?
Action, Horror, Comedy?
That one about the boy?

I'd recognise the name of it,
(Or maybe it's too late?)
Thumbing through the index,
There're so many mistakes.

Countless entries blotted out,
Movies from the past.
It's buried in there somewhere but
The library is vast.

Crystal clear fidelity,
Wrap-around,
Surround,
3D,
An endless vault of memories.
It's getting hard to choose.

A myriad characters portrayed,
Acting, on a common stage.
Performance of a lifetime's age.
Sit back, relax, enjoy.

# Electrocution

Hey, don't snatch!
You know it's rude.
You're gripping me, too tight.
A shocking introduction,
To the stuff that lights the lights.

As if a jagged dagger,
Is stabbing through my spine.
It's agony to turn my head,
But the killer's not behind.

Nerves and muscles, burn with pain.
Bones feel like they'll snap.
I can't release my fingers,
To escape this deadly trap.

As time runs out, I try to shout,
No breath to make a sound.
My vision starts to tunnel.
There's nobody around.

Entombed in darkness,
Death Revealed,
Attacking first, I FIGHT!

A shocking introduction,
To the stuff that lights the lights.

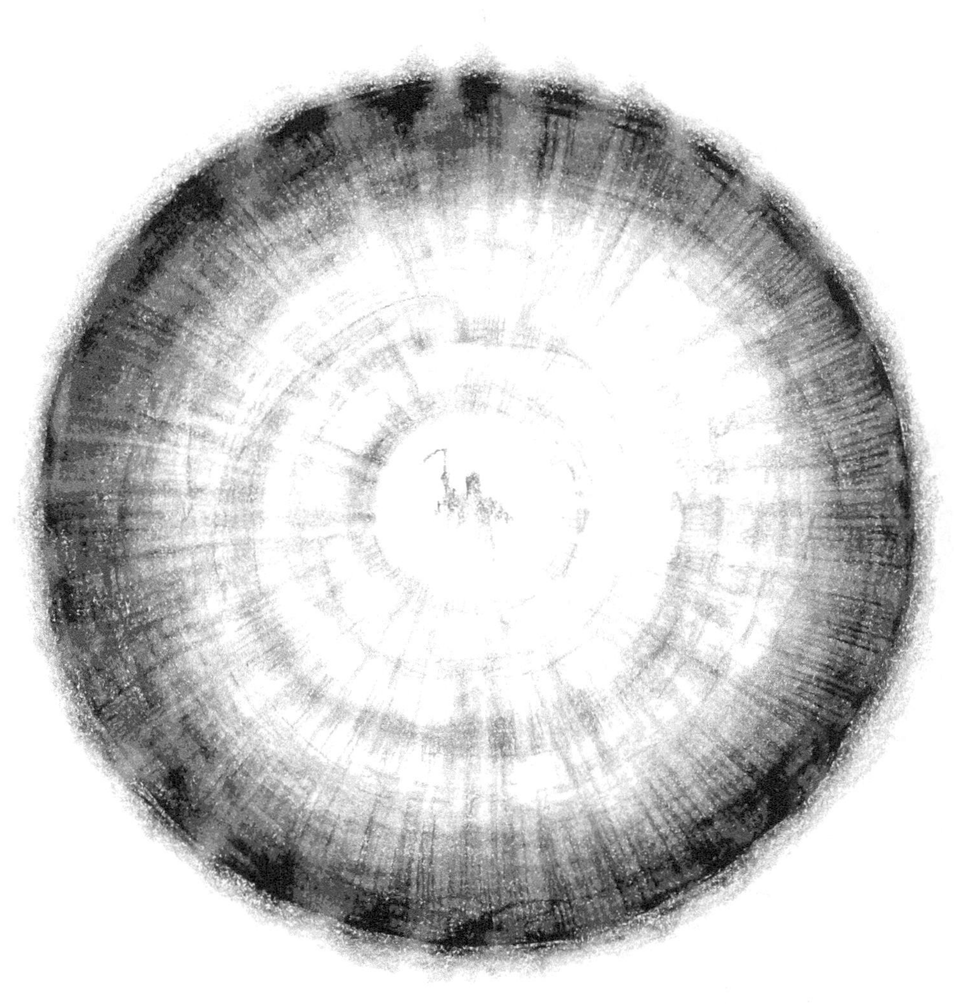

*I think I was nine at the time, just a kid,*
*When I became part of the National Grid*

49

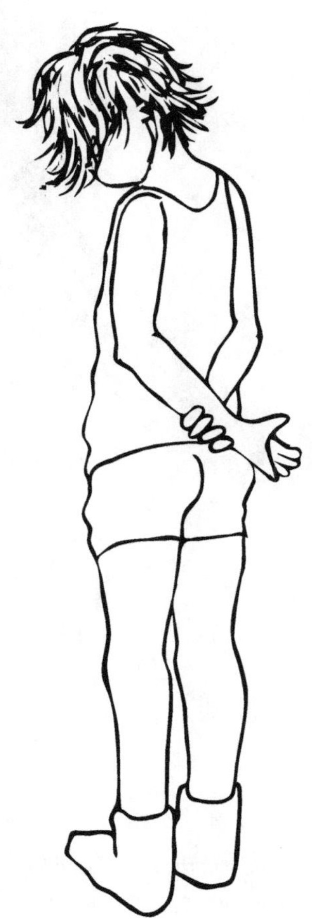

# Primary School

Today's the day they think I'm deaf,
That's right, I cannot hear?!
I'm taken to the office and
Have 'Beeps' played in my ears.

Before that it was reading,
Their lists remained unread.
They should have made the books they gave,
Interesting instead.

Then there was the line-up.
The doctor, pants and vest.
All was fine until my time...
Obstinate protest.

The other kids were not like me,
In fantasy I thrived.
Snapshots, from behind the mask,
At the grand old age of five.

# Naughty

Would you like another one?
No, I think I'll pass.
Just for that, smart answer,
A belt across the arse.

A belt, a stick; I have to pick,
The instrument of pain.
Is this supposed to make me learn?
It's driving me insane.

You WILL do what you're told, or else!
Or else what? Please tell.
Explanations really help,
I lose you when you yell.

I haven't got the hang of this.
I don't know what you need.
I'm learning, as I make mistakes,
The scars that last don't bleed.

There's more to me than meets the eye,
I know you'd understand.
You'd find that Reason, gets results,
Smarter than the hand.

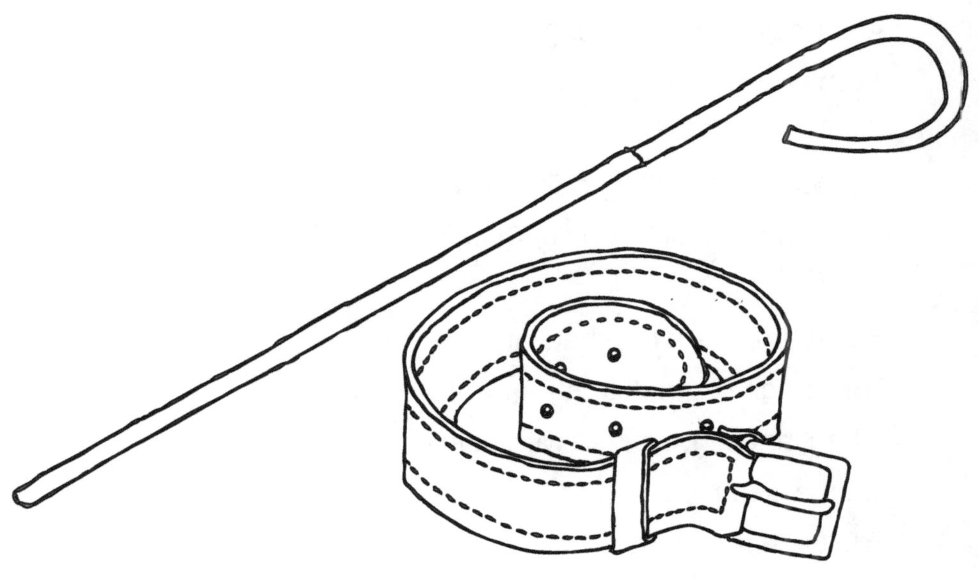

# Education

Way back when I was a kid,
The one thing my school never did,
Was teach me how, to really learn.
It wasn't through a lack of yearning,
Or a lack of interest.
I'm sure the teachers, tried their best.

But even they'd resort to force,
(That lesson, long before, was taught)
And so I learned to hide away,
The fear that greeted every day.
And bit by bit I built a wall,
Of crumbling bricks and alcohol,
And soon a Castle, Man-at-arms,
Alert to any false alarm,
And finally a fuse, so long,
To mask the most destructive bomb.

*Lay Waste the Earth and Salt the Wounds,*
*And Bring the Harbingers of Doom!*

But getting back to school again,
The lesson lies in this refrain.
When innocence is met with pain,
Shame is born,
Trust is slain.

# Cats

I collared next door's tortoiseshell,
Quizzed Felix up the road,
Old Ginger Tom, he gets about,
I wonder what he knows?

But not a single, feline one,
Had got, or even *seen*, my tongue.

For that's a phrase I'd often hear,
When struggling for words,
That won't appear.

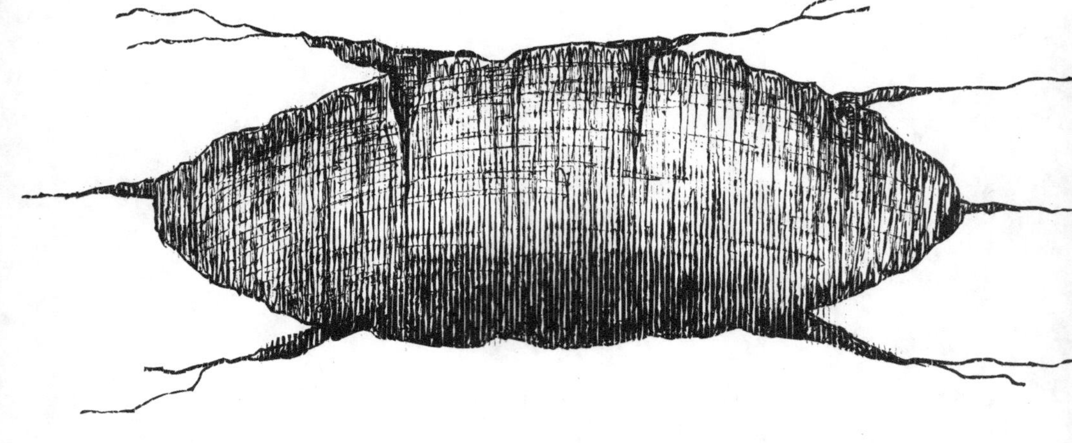

# Pit of Silence

If something has a lot of iron,
Is it irony?
Can puns be used to dilute pain,
To make that pain, puny?

Those funny ways that language works,
Its broken rules and little quirks,
That help to move the message on,
In every nation's native tongue.

But words can fail,
Stutter,
Stall.
Not be suitable at all.
They can't convey a mental map,
They're two dimensional and flat.
In real-time they rarely work,
To practised answers I'll revert.
Which often falter, when recalled;

The pit of silence swallows all.

# Autist

I'm getting told I'm getting old,
I grew up long before,
Autism was a 'real' thing,
And so it was ignored.

A life in isolation, never knowing what to do,
Apparent bouts of 'brilliance', that no one else could do.
Everything is obvious, except another heart.
There's no analysis that fits,
And so I fall apart.

And I can't tell you.

61

I know I just rhymed 'do' with 'do'
And kind of broke the poet's rule
But that's the sort of thing you see
When cursed with this ability

# Over-thinking

If I think I think like I
Think thinking is a thing that I've
Sort of thought I think I knew
I like to think I've thought things through

I loved to think of thoughts of you

I think I thought you'd think the same
Until you stopped
And thought again

# Fool

There is a sense of humour,
I don't quite understand.
Maybe it's a language thing,
It's from another land.

"Szívem örök szerelme" *
A tragic comic irony.
The English form of the words above,
Translates to "My eternal love"

It's funny for it isn't true,
And comedy just loves a fool.
For fools they fall in love with ease.
Those funny fools on fallen knees.

With the punch-line comes the end,
We'll be apart but 'still be friends'.
And for the moment I'll pretend,
That these are tears of joy.

** see-vem oo-rook ser-el-me*

# Broken

Be careful where you put your feet
I haven't got around to sweep
Away the fragments of my life
Shattered by my loving wife.

# Perspectives

"I see it and say it is so", so he said,

While missing the point of this poem.

But he couldn't ignore,

What was outside the door,

And how keenly it wanted to show him.


He turned and he looked and he blinked and he gulped,

Then he frowned as he sauntered away.

And never again would he say what he'd seen,

When he saw that it wasn't the same.

4
5
6
8

# Autistic

I've tried to find and live a life,
As normal as can be,
Because I've seen the way we act,
To people such as me.

If I had a fractured leg,
Or arm in plaster cast,
Then issues would be obvious,
There'd be no need to ask.

But help is scarce for hidden woes,
And so the isolation grows,
Until all thoughts of reaching out,
Have twisted into fear and doubt,
And no-one wants to be the one,
To be the victim,
Overcome.

Most of us, we all belong,

We all

We turn to friends, when things go wrong.

But some of us,

Just can't.

# Sleeping Rough

An empty barn on a disused farm,
Was shelter for a while,
With bales for a bed, I'd rest my head,
Beneath the stars in style.

For these were stars of luxury,
Compared to where I used to be.
Railway stations, after dark,
Were left unlocked, unlike the park.
(Be warned, for when you fall asleep,
The night-trains come and steal your heat.)

But still it was the sanest choice,
The judgement of the inner voice,
The calculations of the risk,
Decided by that final fist.
And all the fault was mine to take,
I was the source of all mistakes.

And so I gave them all thier wish,
I buggered off and bit my lip,
And single-handedly I've tried,
To do the right thing,
(And survive)

I've faced the fear of the great unknown,
Embraced the emptiness, alone.

# Homeless

The stars are really bright tonight.
Those distant suns,
Beacons of light.

I see them through the many gaps,
Between the ageing, wooden slats,
That made a roof, in years gone by.
Now they let in all the sky.

It needs repairs, not sympathy,
This barn is just the place for me.
It's easier for everyone,
As I map out those distant suns.

But cloudless skies reveal a cost,
When morning dew succumbs to frost.
That empty, frozen, forlorn dawn,
Those distant suns, can never warm.

# Astronomology

"This mental instability,
Can it be carried in your genes?"
The question my wife asked of me,
Just before she left.

The sun, once bright, collapsed and died.
Perhaps that's why my love was blind?
And shadows cast in history,
Were all it seemed that she could see.

She couldn't see beyond the mess,
The attributes which I possess,
Like stars in daylight, out of sight,
Only visible at night?
I guess you need to look, to see,
How beautiful the sky can be.

As from this random mess of lights,

That burn beyond this earthly night,

You'll find that figures will emerge,

A hunter roaming, on the verge,

To fight, with club and shield in hand.

There an archer, proudly stands.

A virgin looks with naïve eyes,

As diamonds are transmogrified,

Into an arcing, poison tail,

Each an aspect, or portrayal.

A mimic of complexity,

That lives behind the mess you see.

# Schrödinger's Human

If you look, there's nothing wrong,
I'm six foot four and (fairly) strong.
Talk to me and I'll reply,
I'll even meet you, eye to eye.
Expressions from another face,
Reinforce this carapace.

You see, I've mastered mimicry,
To help maintain 'normality'.
You wouldn't like the real me,
He's friendly, but he's 'odd'.

"Well everybody must pretend..."
That hopeless phrase from those with friends.
But have you ever smashed your head,
Against a wall and begged for death,
Or leapt in front of speeding cars,
Or lived in exile under stars?

I've learned to deal with these attacks,
This mask's a maze of flaws and cracks,
You only see them when you're close,
And that's the time they hurt the most.

I'm like that cat that's in its box,
With poison gas, securely locked.
Alive or barely clinging on?
But if you look, there's nothing wrong.

*Waves will ebb and flow and crash,*
*And when observed, they too, collapse.*

# Suicide

Why do I hide, my suicide?
I have to keep it locked inside,
But never let it out of sight.
It's just part of me.

It's not a subject I can share,
Those darkest thoughts transposed to air.
A slice of soul I cannot bare.
So hidden, it remains.

I know it's hard for you to hear,
Those selfish words, concealing fear,
And so I keep those demons near.
To shelter you from harm.

But demons left un-exorcised,
Will twist and grow and slowly rise,
Consuming all which they despise.
NOTHING WILL SURVIVE...

Why *do* I hide, my suicide?

*Find a professional.*
*Talk about it.*
*If they don't get it, find another one.*
*Don't stop. Don't give up.*

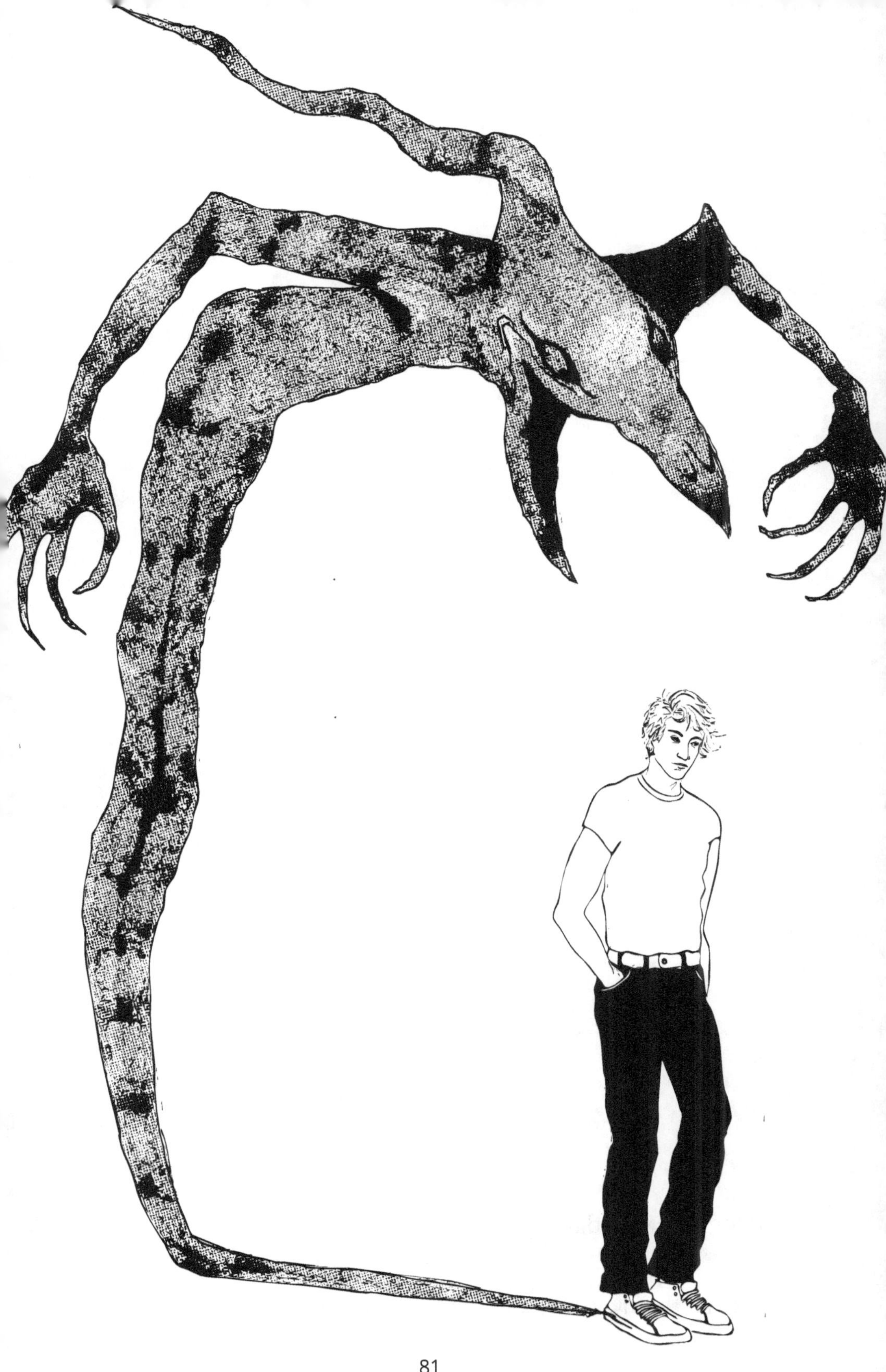

Photograph - 'Bridge'

Sitting by the river, the full moon was so bright. It was beautiful.

It's hard sometimes,
I know, to find,
The fortitude to fight.

But look up from that dark abyss,
Dig Deep,
For brighter shines the light.

# Tsk

That micro-second noise you made,

That passed you by but sealed my fate,

Was softer than a baby's breath,

But lethal, like the scythe of Death.

A thousand people wouldn't hear,

The throwing of that toxic spear.


Now you've got it off your chest,

And plunged it into mine, you rest.

As poison creeps from heart to mind,

Its acid fingers probe to find,

The darkest corners, where it stays,

To lurk behind its barricade.

# Stigma

Not because of damages, nor criminal intent?

This tar-brushing mentality,

Is hard not to resent.

Discrimination of this kind,

Is subtle and it creeps,

It reinforces ignorance,

Through internet repeats.

And this is why it's always hard,
Admitting when I'm weak.
This media bombardment,
Blocks the refuge that I seek.

And so I keep my head down,
I'm in the trench with you.
We soldier on together, but
You're sniping at me too.

# Social Outcast

Social outcast,
Often shunned,
Constant threats to overcome.
Intolerance at every turn,
A life of heavy lessons,
Learnt!

Over time, all feelings die,
Until there's nothing left inside.
The Hope that used to burn within,
Creates a void,
As it grows dim.
Shadows fall where friends should be,
Throw-away society.

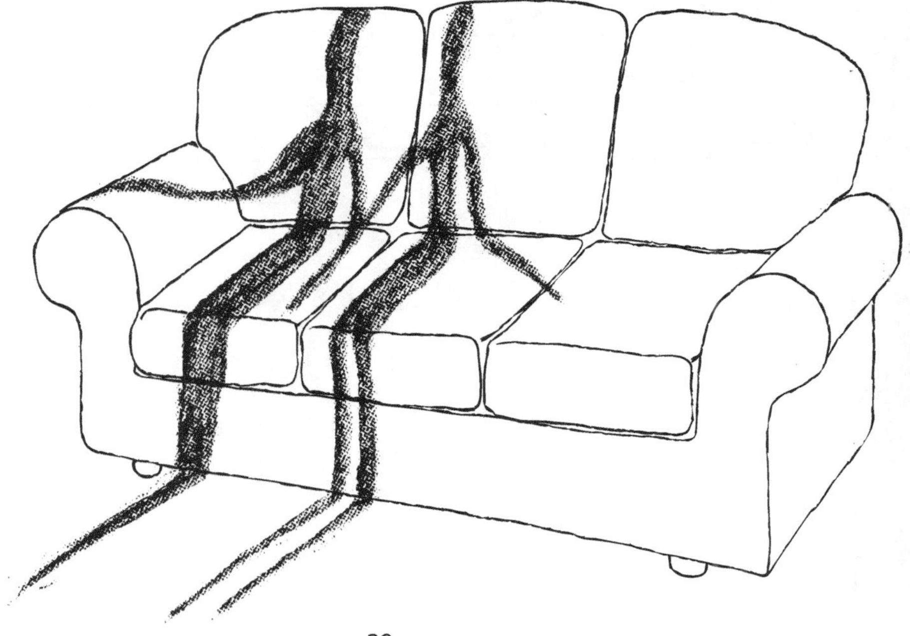

# Summer

The midday sun streams, warmly through,
The window pane, to crash into,
A pair of curtains tightly closed.
To match the fabric of my soul.

They fortify my little room,
Affording me a safe cocoon,
Protecting me, pathetically,
From sociable activity.

Outside, there's children's carefree laughs,
With noisy games played on the grass.
That skill they wield with innocence,
Is treated with indifference,
As all the grown-ups gather round,
The barbecue with puzzled frowns.
It's quite a pleasant atmosphere,
The view that I'm allowed from here.

While witnessing these scenes of fun,
I feel like an alien.
Stranded from another place,
Ill-equipped to integrate,
Condemned to watch these summers pass,
Behind this pane, this window glass.

# Alien

Planet: Earth
System: Sol
Atmosphere: Unusual
Target Species: Human Race
Reconciling database:

A task accomplished, easily,
When all the work was done for me.
They harvest knowledge greedily,
With clever new technology.

*An orchard grown from little seeds.*

But still they have that hidden gene,
That terrifies their children's dreams,
And turns them into war machines.
That echo from the past.

Traits they cannot seem to shake,
Feudal habits, hard to break,
Maybe given time, they'll mend?
To be reviewed.
Transmission ends:

# Favours

"If you got a minute mate,
Me laptop's on the blink."
"It might have got some beer on it,
So I rinsed it, in the sink."

Of course it's fine, just pick a time,
Before The Match but after nine?
(Don't try to guess, you won't be right)
In any case I'm up all night.
I'll see you later, mate.

That bloomin' Sod, his effin' Law,
A red alert!
I'm out the door,
To who knows where, how, why, what for?
I could be quite a while.

Somewhere, someone's clock says 'Eight',
I'm unaware it's getting late.
So when I find that faulty line,
The Match is played, it's Question Time *.

My patient lives!
My work is done.
Elated in the morning sun.
Yet somehow, on the journey home,
The Bluetooth and the telephone,
They suck the fun from everything,
As messages start flooding in.
It sounds like mate, is quite irate.

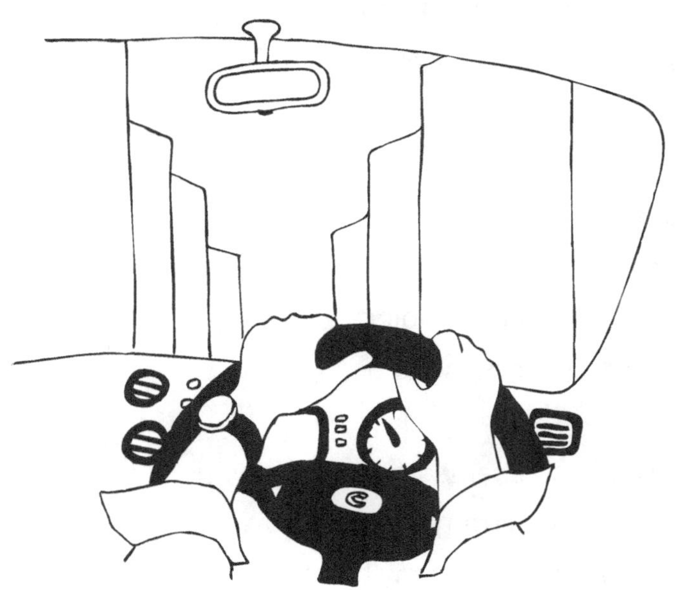

*Question Time was a late night TV programme.*

# Hit Reset

"I've turned it off and on again."
"These damned machines, they are a pain."
It sounds like someone didn't think,
And clicked a
<u>* Claim Your'e Winnings !!! *</u>
Link.

No problem, I appreciate,
How passionately you remonstrate.
Com-pew-ter illiterate.
It's fine, I understand.

Behind the mask, a thousand cuts,
Of senses dulled and knotted guts.
Drowning, in this cloying sea,
Of tedious mediocrity.

This child, whom I've known since birth,
Aware of its potential worth,
For science, and technology,
And anything it chose to be.

This child and I helped pave the way,
That thousands trample, every day.
I need to reach inside my brain,
And turn it off, and on again.

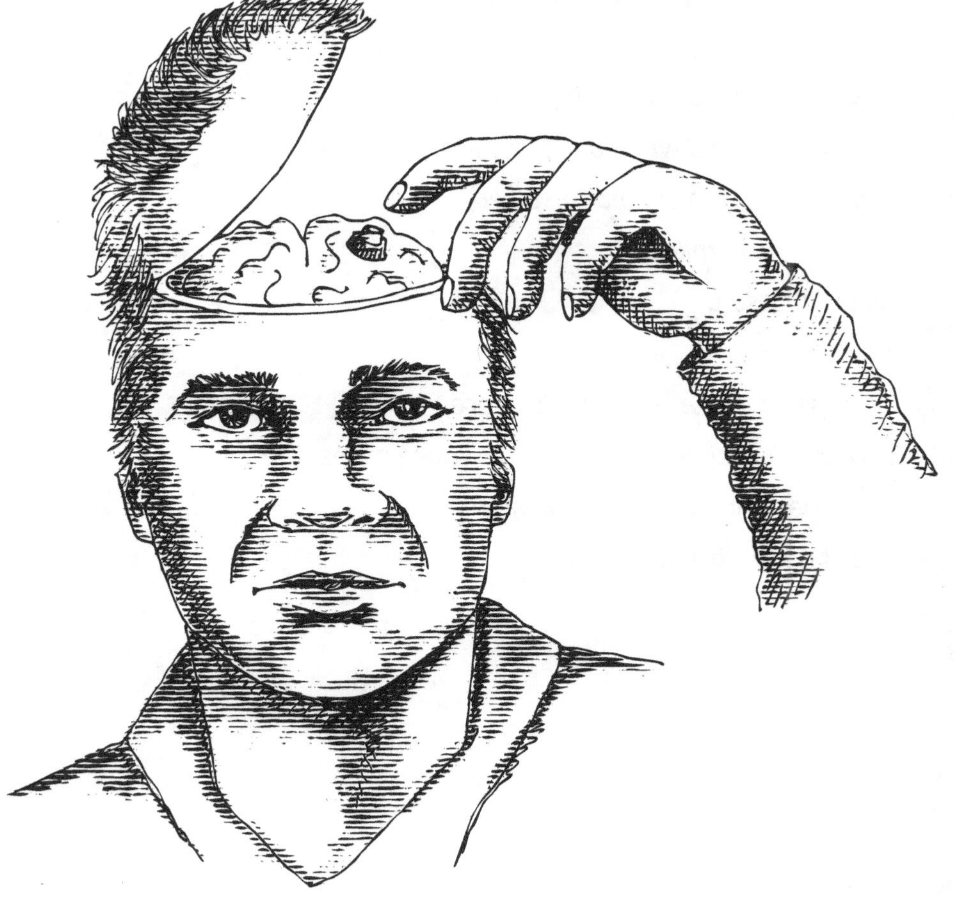

# Patience

"Always optimistic."
"The patience of a saint."
"He never seems to get upset, or flinch at our mistakes."

Endearing things that people say,
When I've turned up and "saved the day",
As nothing seems to aggravate,
Like kit that won't co-operate,
(Computers always seems to 'break',
The *instant* that report is late.)

*Yet, in the midst of much frustration,*
*Faults are fixed with concentration.*
*Sullen faces frowned and sulked,*
*Now happy smiles.*
*A great result.*

You see for me the value's there,
To know that someone, somewhere cares.
And patience is a point of view,
For I have difficulties too.

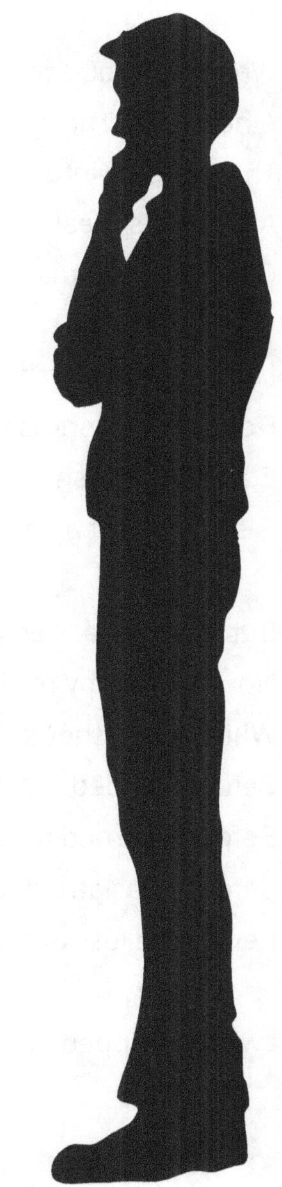

# Reflection

Nip it in the bud,
Before it gets much worse.
An inauspicious start,
For another rambling verse.

What *is* this bud that needs a nip?
A helpful, horticultural tip,
That's grown into a lazy phrase,
And lost its meaning, in the maze,
Of tangled idioms.

I have no roots in botany,
How can this phrase apply to me?
Comparing flesh and bone to tree,
Is stretching it a bit.

But looking back across the years,
Now broken, by my hidden fears,
Which really should have been addressed,
Before I landed in this mess.
Before I learned to wear the mask.
Before I was afraid to ask.
Before the loss of all I've loved,

I wish I'd nipped it, in the bud.

# Hard Man

Look out, he's a 'Hard Man'
He's got tattoos and scars,
He drinks and terrorises,
All the local clubs and bars.

And 'Hard Man' is the term to use,
The bully's badge of pride.
He'll punch you in the face,
Before admitting that he's cried.

*Such visible aggression isn't hard to understand,*
*But real strength stays silent,*
*In bars across the land.*

I know, because I drank alone,
For years, (but not a drop at home)
The pub would help me settle down,
While booze would sooth my inner frown.
And as befits a toxic place,
I've witnessed alcohol's disgrace.

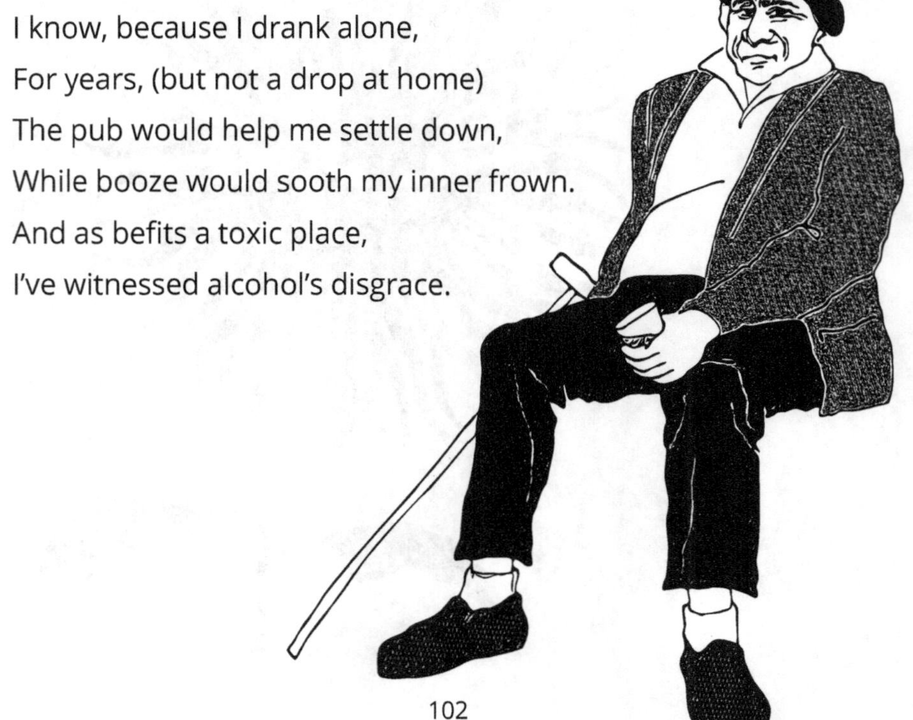

But not all patrons are the same,
For some the drink's a ball and chain,
For others, it's a brief relief,
To numb the grind of daily grief.

Yet still in taverns, up and down,
This land, in strangers, I have found,
Tales that only ales will tell,
To nameless ears of hidden Hells.
You hear of Heroes, tales of strife,
A view of real human life.

An often hidden sense of shame,
For real Hard Men, feel pain.

# Motivations

Stick, carrot; carrot, stick,
Which of these would do the trick,
If you had the chance to pick,
To motivate your day?

Of course the question is absurd,
Without a doubt, we'd choose reward,
But there the rose reveals its thorn,
The carrot feeds a unicorn.

For pleasant things, we're pleased to take,
While snapping off a stick, we break,
To keep the minions in their place,
It's funny how it works.

# Tinnitus

Ten kilohertz,

The frequenc -

eeeeeeeeeeeeeeeeeeeeeeeeeeeeeeeeeeeeeeeeeeeeeeeeeeeeee
eeeeeeeeeeeeeeeeeeeeeeeeeeeeeeeeeeeeeeeeeeeeeeeeeeeeee
eeeeeeeeeeeeeeeeeeeeeeeeeeeeeeeeeeeeeeeeeeeeeeeeeeeeee
eeeeeeeeeeeeeeeeeeeeeeeeeeeeeeeeeeeeeeeeeeeeeeeeeeeeee
eeeeeeeeeeeeeeeeeeeeeeeeeeeeeeeeeeeeeeeeeeeeeeeeeeeeee
eeeeeeeeeeeeeeeeeeeeeeeeeeeeeeeeeeeeeeeeeeeeeeeeeeeeee
eeeeeeeeeeeeeeeeeeeeeeeeeeeeeeeeeeeeeeeeeeeeeeeeeeeeee
eeeeeeeeeeeeeeeeeeeeeeeeeeeeeeeeeeeeeeeeeeeeeeeeeeeeee
eeeeeeeeeeeeeeeeeeeeeeeeeeeeeeeeeeeeeeeeeeeeeeeeeeeeee
eeeeeeeeeeeeeeeeeeeeeeeeeeeeeeeeeeeeeeeeeeeeeeeeeeeeee
eeeeeeeeeeeeeeeeeeeeeeeeeeeeeeeeeeeeeeeeeeeeeeeeeeeeee
eeeeeeeeeeeeeeeeeeeeeeeeeeeeeeeeeeeeeeeeeeeeeeeeeeeeee
eeeeeeeeeeeeeeeeeeeeeeeeeeeeeeeeeeeeeeeeeeeeeeeeeeeeee
eeeeeeeeeeeeeeeeeeeeeeeeeeeeeeeeeeeeeeeeeeeeeeeeeeeeee
eeeeeeeeeeeeeeeeeeeeeeeeeeeeeeeeeeeeeeeeeeeeeeeeeeeeee
eeeeeeeeeeeeeeeeeeeeeeeeeeeeeeeeeeeeeeeeeeeeeeeeeeeeee
eeeeeeeeeeeeeeeeeeeeeeeeeeeeeeeeeeeeeeeeeeeeeeeeeeeeee
eeeeeeeeeeeeeeeeeeeeeeeeeeeeeeeeeeeeeeeeeeeeeeeeeeeeee
eeeeeeeeeeeeeeeeeeeeeeeeeeeeeeeeeeeeeeeeeeeeeeeeeeeeee
eeeeeeeeeeeeeeeeeeeeeeeeeeeeeeeeeeeeeeeeeeeeeeeeeeeeee
eeeeeeeeeeeeeeeeeeeeeeeeeeeeeeeeeeeeeeeeeeeeeeeeeeeeee
eeeeeeeeeeeeeeeeeeeeeeeeeeeeeeeeeeeeeeeeeeeeeeeeeeeeee
eeeeeeeeeeeeeeeeeeeeeeeeeeeeeeeeeeeeeeeeeeeeeeeeeeeeee
eeeeeeeeeeeeeeeeeeeeeeeeeeeeeeeeeeeeeeeeeeeeeeeeeeeeee
eeeeeeeeeeeeeeeeeeeeeeeeeeeeeeeeeeeeeeeeeeeeeeeeeeeeee
eeeeeeeeeeeeeeeeeeeeeeeeeeeeeeeeeeeeeeeeeeeeeeeeeeeeee
eeeeeeeeeeeeeeeeeeeeeeeeeeeeeeeeeeeeeeeeeeeeeeeeeeeeee
eeeeeeeeeeeeeeeeeeeeeeeeeeeeeeeeeeeeeeeeeeeeeeeeeeeeee
eeeeeeeeeeeeeeeeeeeeeeeeeeeeeeeeeeeeeeeeeeeeeeeeeee -y

That never, Ever STOPS!

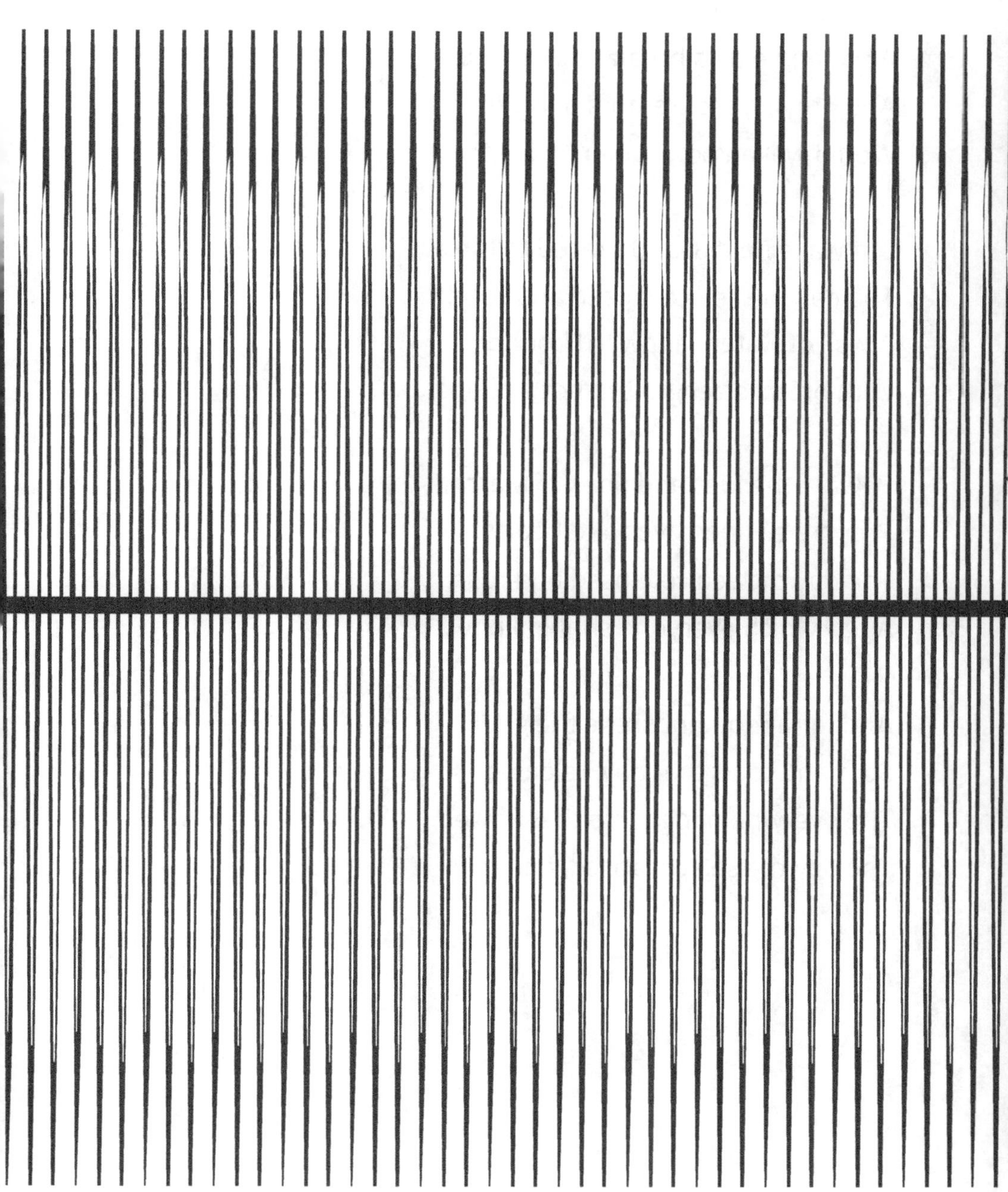

# Tōhoku Tsunami

The day the sea collapsed and rose,
A nation held its breath and hoped,
And prayed, the tremors underfoot,
Would waken not, Ryūjin's * wrath.

But wake he did, and braced to throw,
The day the sea collapsed and rose,
A wall of water, landward bound,
With brutal strength but not a sound.

Beware the ides and tides of March,
Prepare to open eyes and hearts,
The day the sea collapsed and rose,
A day which everyone should know,

And for a moment share the grief,
So many souls that day, released.
The overwhelming force that flowed,
The day the sea collapsed, and rose.

** In Japanese mythology, Ryūjin was the dragon god of the sea.*

# Chernobyl

Back in nineteen eighty-six,
The flicking of a little switch,
Caused a surge, a spike to peak.
That Blasted main reactor leaked.

With isotope polluted skies,
The politicians realised,
We needed, rather rapidly,
A programme, and a team to screen,
For any radio-active cloud,
That taints the grass that feeds the cows.
So there I was, to lend a hand [1],
But what transpired wasn't planned.

Before this programme was deployed,

The government bought lots of toys,

That could detect the smallest trace,

Of any nasty gamma-rays.

But nobody could turn it on,

(You must remember this was long,

Before the days of home PCs,

And 'common knowledge' of IT)

But when that cursor winked at me,

I found the main commands with ease.

A kind of custom CP/M [2].

(There wasn't any Windows® then)

And pretty soon I'd programmed in,

The scripts that made the sensors sing.


A second thought, I never gave,

Now over half a life away.

A point in time of consequence,

A chain-reaction of events.

Fate, or just coincidence?

At the flicking, of a switch.

*1 - Working primarily as an analytical chemist, my background, interest and knowledge of computers was instrumental in getting computers adopted by government laboratories.*

*2 - CP/M – Control Program for Microcomputers. An early operating system.*

# Bouncer

Another funny thing I've done,
Or rather, had to do,
I was a nightclub doorman,
Certificated too.

I had a knack for picking out,
The trouble-makers in a crowd,
And with a smile I'd intervene,
Before they could create a scene.

Of course it came with many risks,
The violent, angry, armed, and pissed.
All were dealt a poker-face,
On hand I'd stand to keep you safe.

And sure I've had my share of spills,
I've paid with blood to pay the bills,
But I'd choose humour, to amuse,
A friendly ear to help defuse,
Any spark of dissonance,
Or alcohol-fuelled ignorance.

*When trouble isn't left behind, trouble follows troubled minds.*

And so revealed the paradox,
The leper, shepherding the flocks.
Working while you're having fun,
Alert to all, but close to none.

Photograph - 'Lion'

Carved wood lion (by Seamus Cuddihy) seen during an occupational therapy, art gallery, outing.

You'll never notice from afar,
This mask's a maze of flaws and scars.
You'll only see them when you're close,
And that's the time they hurt the most.

# Pavlovian

"There's nothing solved by worrying",
Another helpful quip.
Apparently it just involves,
A series of, 'What if...'s.

So, 'what if' all this apprehension,
Restlessness and dread;
Is simply a reaction,
To the knowledge in my head?

Wisdom earned from battles lost,
A map of scars, the heavy cost.
Pitfalls lurking in the dark,
Which way to go?
No voice to ask.

Imagine all those thoughts inside,
All sensations multiplied,
Computations running wild,
And nobody can see.

For ever, with the best intent,
I cannot let this quest relent,
And cave to thoughts of giving in.
There's nothing solved by worrying.

THIS WAY
THAT WAY

# Counselling

With so much damning evidence,
So many clues, does my defence,
Rely on such a simple plea?
It was my friend, Insanity.

For each transgression, I attest,
I've always strived to do the best,
For Everybody Else's good.
My friend has always understood.

A diatribe of how I've tried,
Of secret trials, past denied.
The hand of Justice, often cruel,
Objections staying overruled,
The nights that never seemed to end,
In solitary, with my friend.

And while the jury's out to vote,
These revelations kindle hopes,
That maybe yet we could be free,
A final chance of amnesty?
Release the shackles binding me,
Release my friend, Insanity.

Photograph - 'Waterfall'

Not everything comes easy.

AMIDST A RAGING WATERFALL,
THIS LITTLE PLANT I FOUND.
AND I WAS MOVED BY HOW IT GREW,
WITH CHAOS ALL AROUND.

# Acknowledgements

## Liane Matthews

Primarily a ceramicist, I met Liane when she was tutoring an occupational therapy pottery class (pottery is great fun, do try it). She also does printmaking, drawing, sketches, a very talented lady. In return for taking photographs of some of her ceramic pieces, I asked if she would be interested in doing the illustrations for "Why Poetry?" and she said "Yes, ok".

It was an interesting time as, until then, I hadn't shared the poetry outside the circle of therapy professionals. She was very kind in her review of it and I think she's done a wonderful job of capturing the spirit of the poems with her drawings.

You can find Liane's works at her website:

www.lianematthews.com

# About the Author

## Nigel Johnston

At first glance you might see Nigel as a normal, friendly, albeit quiet individual.

Scratch the surface and you'll soon get to the quirky layers.

Dig a little deeper and you'll uncover a fantastic world of science, technology, music, photography and creativity; all built upon a foundation of desperate struggles and hardships.

As many did, Nigel grew up in a time before autism was widely recognised and as such, blundered into every pitfall of the autistic traits. Nowadays he's a lot more forgiving of himself and spends his time in nature taking photographs.

You can see some of Nigel's photos and other writings at his website:

www.nigeljohnston.com

This page is intentionally blank

*I know it's just a silly thing,*
*But that, up there,*
*It always brings a grin.*